Homeschool Curriculum That's Effective and Fun!

Avoid the Crummy Curriculum Hall of Shame

D1456512

Lee Binz,
The HomeScholar

First Printing, 2015

Printed in the United States of America

ISBN: 1508999341
ISBN-13: 978-1508999348

Disclaimer: Parents assume full responsibility for the education of their children in accordance with state law. College requirements vary, so make sure to check with the colleges about specific requirements for homeschoolers. We offer no guarantees, written or implied, that the use of our products and services will result in college admissions or scholarship awards.

Homeschool Curriculum That's Effective and Fun!

Avoid the Crummy Curriculum Hall of Shame

What are
Coffee Break Books?

Homeschool Curriculum That's Effective and Fun is part of The HomeScholar's Coffee Break Book series.

Designed especially for parents who don't want to spend hours and hours reading a 400-page book on homeschooling high school, each book combines Lee's practical and friendly approach with detailed, but easy-to-digest information, perfect to read over a cup of coffee at your favorite coffee shop!

Never overwhelming, always accessible and manageable, each book in the series will give parents the tools they need to tackle the tasks of homeschooling high school, one warm sip at a time.

Everything about these Coffee Break Books is designed to suggest simplicity, ease and comfort - from the size (fits in a purse), to the font and paragraph length (easy on the eyes), to the price (the same as a Starbucks Venti Triple Caramel Macchiato). Unlike a fancy coffee drink, however, these books are guilt-free pleasures you will want to enjoy again and again!

Table of Contents

Introduction

No One-Size Fits All Curriculum

One of the most common questions I'm asked is what curriculum I recommend. Alas, I do not have the perfect one-size-fits-all recommendation for anyone, because we're all different and our children are all different! The best way I can answer this question is to encourage you to find a curriculum that's effective – one that works for you and is also fun (or at least as close to fun as we can get with our children)! I recognize there are way too many wonderful choices out there in the world of curriculum for me to make recommendations for everyone.

In years past, homeschoolers didn't have many choices when it came to curriculum, but now our community is so large that publishers flood the market with hundreds of options. On one hand, this abundance is great but there are too many options! You cannot use all the good curriculum out there.

In the following pages, I will discuss general strategies for choosing a curriculum. I'll describe the different homeschool approaches and talk about the different learning styles for both children and parents. We'll spend some time on the current fads, fears, and pressures homeschool parents and kids feel. I'll also give some subject-specific suggestions and fun schooling ideas that might help if you need some encouragement.

We'll conclude with money matters such as how to afford curriculum and we'll look at some resources that can help. Through it all, we'll discuss how to maintain sanity with some real world, sanity-saving ideas. We'll try to keep the focus on balance and sanity so these ideas will work for you. Let's go!

Chapter 1

Stick with What Works

The most important general strategy for choosing curriculum is to stick with the curriculum that works. When you identify something that works (whether it's baking brownies at the end of a hard workday or sipping a latte to get started in the morning), that's what you need to do in order to survive. A curriculum is like that, too; use what works.

If your homeschool curriculum has been working all along, keep using it; stick with it and don't make a change. No matter how green the grass is on the other side of the fence, you have no guarantee the shiny new curriculum is going to work. All you know for sure is your current curriculum is working for your child. Even if another curriculum works great for your best friend's kids that doesn't mean it will work for you.

A second important strategy is to use the method that works. If you use a learning style or a homeschooling style that works, keep using it. If you're doing great with delight directed learning, stick with it. If you use the school-at-home approach and your kid thrives on textbooks and workbooks, then keep at it. The flip side of this is also true. If the approach you are taking is not working, then stop using it and either go back to what you used before or make a change. Look for a curriculum provider that has worked for you in the past.

I personally used *Sonlight* curriculum. When they recommended a resource, I knew there was a high likelihood it would be successful for us because everything else they recommended was successful. If you find something that works, keep using it, whether it's a curriculum, a style, or a provider. (If all else fails, grab some chocolate because chocolate solves all of life's problems.)

Use Homeschool Curriculum

One of my most important guidelines is to choose a homeschool curriculum whenever possible. Homeschool curriculum is quite different from public school curriculum. It assumes the teacher knows nothing about the subject. If you choose a public school curriculum, it may assume you have a degree in the subject in order to teach it. Homeschool parents don't typically have knowledge in all possible subjects and homeschool curriculum makes allowances for this. Homeschool curriculum is also intended to work well at home rather than in a group setting with group questions and group activities.

When my sons were in high school, I was nervous about teaching them Latin. I knew nothing about Latin. I had one Latin book I borrowed from a friend, downloaded a sample from another Latin curriculum, and compared the two of them. I was a bit shocked when I looked at my friend's book; after looking at the first page, I didn't have a clue what it was talking about! If I'd used that book, I wouldn't have known how to instruct my children. It was definitely intended for a public school setting, because it assumed I knew Latin. In contrast, the first chapter of the homeschool Latin program said, "Copy this information into your own notebook so you will learn what Latin is." So that's what we did. This book gave specific directions for what to do each day and I can say with confidence that my sons learned Latin.

As homeschoolers, we try to save money and sometimes we're desperate enough to grab a used textbook from the public school. That won't help in the long run. It may not even save you money if the book gets so frustrating that your child ends up hating the subject.

As a homeschool teacher, you don't need to have a degree in order to teach a subject. One of the goals for homeschooling is to teach our children how to learn. When you use a homeschool curriculum, make sure it's one that promotes self-teaching. Children need to learn how to learn; it's one of the most important skills we can teach our children, both for college and for life.

Adults need to teach themselves all the time. I had to teach myself how to use the computer (but my husband helped!). I had to teach myself how to use QuickBooks. Self-teaching is what adults do in their day-to-day life. Children will grow up and become adults who need to teach themselves. When you use a self-teaching curriculum, you're training your children to become better adults – it's an important skill for adulthood.

In the younger years, parents are more of a teacher. We teach our children how to write in cursive, multiply, and understand historical events. When children become teenagers, they start self-teaching more and more. That's when the parent's role changes from teacher to project manager — the overseer, who simply makes sure it's done correctly, but doesn't do the work.

This is one reason you don't have to learn Latin or physics in order to teach it. You only have to be the project manager for your child.

Public schools don't usually have the benefit of using a homeschool curriculum and sometimes teachers don't even have a degree in the subject they teach. If you feel inadequate, just remember that all teachers struggle with the same challenges. Sometimes even gifted teachers with a degree have difficulty teaching when forced to use a rotten curriculum. As a homeschool parent, you get to choose a curriculum you feel comfortable using, regardless of whether you have a degree in the subject. You can also use a curriculum that is appropriate for your children and make as many modifications as needed as time goes on. What freedom!

Chapter 2

Encourage Progress and Invest in Weaknesses

When considering your curriculum from year to year, focus on encouraging your child's forward progress. Focus on the learning that occurs, not whether you finish the curriculum. If you change curriculum, you don't have to start at the beginning.

Some curriculum manufacturers say that if you change to their math program, you need to start at the beginning because your child has gaps to fill. The problem is that if you keep starting over with a brand new curriculum, your child could end up studying Pre-Algebra forever!

I've met parents who were concerned their child didn't have a thorough understanding of Pre-Algebra, so they tried a different Pre-Algebra program the next year to see if it would work. The child still didn't achieve perfection in the subject, so they tried yet another curriculum for Pre-Algebra the next year!

A student doesn't have to reach perfection! When a child completes the curriculum, they probably have learned enough and are ready to move forward even if they haven't mastered it perfectly.

If this is one of your concerns, consider giving a pretest before you start using a new curriculum, especially for subjects such as math that have progressive information. A pretest can determine whether your student needs to start in Algebra 1 or Pre-Algebra.

I encourage you to know your child and trust yourself. You have a much better understanding of what your child is ready for and what they should do next than a curriculum provider who says you need to start over. I can give you encouragement and suggestions, but I'm not the authority on your child. You are the authority; you're the only one who knows all of the information. Trust yourself. Many parents discount their own gut instinct. Usually your gut feeling is honest and true.

As you encourage forward momentum, also encourage specialization. Help your child do what they like to do — interests and abilities unique to your child. Make sure you don't schedule every moment of their day, though. You don't want to teach eight classes of high school five days a week. Your child will be miserable and won't have time to find unique interests.

Allow time for your child to discover their own specialization. Colleges call this passion – they love to see it or anything unique about a child. I usually call this delight directed learning, when the child is interested in learning about their favorite topic. Encouraging specialization is important and worth pursuing.

Invest in Weaknesses

As homeschool parents, we need to recognize and be honest about our own areas of weaknesses. Areas of strength, both our children's and ours, are things that tend to take care of themselves. If you have a child who's a natural artist, they will probably have art supplies all over the house. You won't need to throw money and time into learning art because it will take care of itself naturally. If you personally are an artist, you will have art materials all over the house and won't need to invest in art. Instead, invest in your weaknesses. First invest in your student's area of weakness, but also invest in your own.

There are two ways to invest in weaknesses. Put your weaknesses first in terms of your time. The area your child struggles with is the area they should work on first. Have your child study their weak subject in the morning, right after breakfast, when they're fresh and have energy, not in the late afternoon when they're too tired. It's the first thing they should do each day. Don't let them do something else when they should be working on that one subject. No matter what comes up, do that subject first — even if it's Super Bowl tickets! Don't go to that event until you have finished the weak subject area.

The second way to invest in your weakness is to put your weak area first in terms of money. Your weak area should be the first place where you spend your curriculum dollars. Most homeschool families have a budget, and it's not usually a limitless pot of money! Identify what your child isn't completing in your homeschool or your own weak area as a teacher. If a curriculum hasn't been working, and it's your weak area, that's where you must be willing to re-invest. If a math program isn't working and math is your child's weak area, buy another math book. Start over and get math done.

Also invest in yourself and your vocation as a homeschool parent. Consider your own continuing education. Buy books about homeschooling that will help you with record keeping or college admission. I encourage parents to take classes about how to homeschool high school. That's why I like to see parents attend conventions. By going to a convention each year, you can learn more about homeschooling.

Chapter 3

Searching for the Perfect Curriculum

One of the problems with looking for a curriculum that's fun is we're tempted to search for the so-called perfect curriculum. Perfection doesn't exist; you won't find it anywhere except in the Lord! If you search for the perfect curriculum, I can guarantee you're not going to find it because it's an illusion. Instead, focus on tried and true curriculum. You're more likely to find a curriculum that works, fits, and will see you through beginning to end if it's a tried and true curriculum used by other homeschoolers.

The opposite of tried and true is the latest and greatest curriculum.

Sometimes a new curriculum can look fabulous and you might even think it will be a great fit and give it a try. Other times it's simply an unproven fad – something you're not sure will work. One of the biggest problems with looking at the latest and greatest curriculum is sometimes the curriculum isn't quite finished. It's not uncommon for a curriculum provider to plan a 4-year history program and you buy the first two years but when you're ready for the third year, it isn't available yet.

When possible, put greater value on a curriculum that's been around the block a few times. Pick a curriculum that has been used by other homeschoolers, (whose reviews have been around for a while). This way you know what you're going to get over a curriculum that might be the latest and greatest but is unproven. A tried and true curriculum can often be cheaper than a new curriculum. If a curriculum has been around for a while, there's a higher likelihood of finding a used copy or a used past edition instead of the latest edition.

Remember that the grass isn't always greener on the other side! Just because your curriculum isn't perfect, and you are searching for a perfect curriculum, doesn't mean you're going to find one. The one you're thinking of buying may not be any better than what you own. If yours is working, keep using it. If your child likes a curriculum, they will learn more from it. If they hate a curriculum, they will learn less from it.

Feedback from Teens

One math curriculum is the highest rated (*Saxon Math*). The problem is that some kids (and parents) absolutely hate it! If your child uses a top rated program and hates it so much they only learn 70% of what they should have learned, it won't work! If they use a less highly rated program but like it and learn, they might come out smarter. Your child's preferences need to be factored into your decision when you choose a curriculum.

Sometimes teenagers use a bullhorn when they give you feedback. Other times you'll have to lean in and listen carefully, especially with quieter kids. It can be difficult for them to provide feedback to Mom and Dad. It's important to allow teens to choose when they're interested or able to choose. Kids have some personal preferences we can't understand. They might have pet peeves or quirks which are likely to be the complete opposite of your own opinions.

For example, most math curriculum have a video tutorial. If your child is to be successful in math, it will help if you look at video tutorials together side by side. Your child might have a personal preference, a quirk you have never identified. I've talked to teens who say they hate a video because a southern accent drove them crazy or they couldn't understand the way a teacher talked. One teen thought the man in their video tutorial was creepy. As a parent, you might not be able to look at a video and determine that the teacher will look creepy to your child!

Some teenagers scoff at a black board, while others *strongly* prefer a white board. Some want to see a real person in a video tutorial so they can see facial expressions. These personal preferences can have a big impact on whether or not a student is successful. This is especially important in your student's weak areas.

I encourage you to look at samples online with your student. Most books have online samples. You can go to Amazon.com and check out the "Look Inside" feature to view a few pages and see whether you like how it is written. You can also attend a convention and look at curriculum in person.

When I was homeschooling, we had to choose a new curriculum for Algebra 2. I was a little concerned, because at that point, there weren't many wonderful options. I thought I was stuck with *Saxon*, which I personally had a huge bias against. My nephew is a calculus teacher at a public school, and he told me *Saxon* is the highest rated program, and that he used *Saxon* math when he was in college getting his degree in math. Yet my personal preference was not to use it.

I didn't know which curriculum to choose for Algebra 2, and when I got stuck I had to get some input from my teenagers. I was shocked when my oldest son looked at the *Saxon* math book and thought it was the coolest thing in the world. He loved having all those problems on the page, without any of those crazy, annoying (to him!) pictures throughout the whole textbook. I would never have thought that was a positive thing to look for in a math book. I always looked for math books with great pictures, so my son's reaction didn't make any sense to me! But that was my teen's preference. By listening to him, we purchased a curriculum that was a good fit and he was able to learn more. Get feedback from your teens when you can.

I'm also a realist, and I have to say that while my son did give me feedback on *Saxon* math, there were 88 other areas where I asked him to give me feedback on curriculum and he frankly wasn't interested; he couldn't care less! If that's the case, recognize that you cannot force an opinion out of your child. If they don't have an opinion, then you get to choose and they don't get to complain!

Chapter 4

Homeschool Approaches

A homeschool curriculum should always find a balance between being too uptight and too relaxed; that may mean something different for your family than it did for mine. If people looked at my homeschool curriculum, many would likely think it was uptight. In my homeschool, I used an uptight curriculum, but in a relaxed way.

There are many different homeschool approaches out there, just as there are many different kinds of parents. Some parents are relaxed and others have many rules and different opinions on parenting. Homeschool approaches can range from unschooling to classical schooling, with everything in between. There also tends to be a tie-in between homeschool approaches and parenting approaches. Some of the choices parents make aren't about homeschooling at all – they're parenting choices. Let's look at some of the most common homeschool approaches.

School-at-Home

The school-at-home approach imitates a public or private school in many ways, utilizing primarily textbooks and workbooks. This method uses different books for each grade level, specific to each grade. Video tutorials are often set in a classroom to give even more of that school-at-home feel. It can involve lesson plans, attendance records, and even saluting the flag every morning.

School-at-home homeschoolers often have a schoolroom or school desks set up in their homes. Beginning homeschoolers are the most likely to set aside a schoolroom, line up desks, and place a flag in the corner. It usually doesn't take long for homeschoolers to realize they don't need to imitate school; not all parts of a brick and mortar school are worth imitating. This approach can be appealing for beginners, but it's not an approach I recommend. Instead, I think it's better to make a complete break from school and separate your style from school-at-home as much as possible, to help instill the love of learning in your children.

It's important to free yourself in some ways from the idea of being a teacher. You don't need to be a teacher – you don't even have to play a teacher on TV. You don't have to be certified and you don't have to have a college degree in order to be successful. If you pulled your children out of public or private school for a reason, if school didn't work for your children, don't imitate it at home. That said, I know school-at-home is a style many homeschoolers use. I encourage people to use what works, so if it works for you, stick with it.

Literature-based

There is a variety of different ways to incorporate literature-based education into your homeschool. One of the first that comes to mind is using the popular Classical approach. It focuses on training great minds using critical thinking skills, logic, and rhetoric. The Socratic method is used for discussion. Often there's an emphasis on learning Latin and reading the classics. This can be an intensive education which takes a lot of time. I've seen it be successful for children and I've also seen it fail, just as any other kind of approach can fail. I encourage parents to think long and hard about whether the rigor and intensity of this approach will be a good fit for their children.

Another method is using a living books, literature-based curriculum. One example is the Charlotte Mason approach. Charlotte Mason calls the literature she recommends "twaddle-free," which means they are books with beautiful language and vocabulary, rather than books such as *Clifford the*

Big Red Dog. Read books that are meaningful and challenging, but don't fall into the trap of believing old books are the best or only ones you can read; some older books aren't written terribly well. Charlotte Mason education also encourages nature study and a focus on shorter lessons.

When my children were in public school, the class used a literature-based curriculum; it's not unique to homeschoolers. When I started homeschooling, I desperately wanted to be a Charlotte Mason homeschooler. My children loved living, "twaddle-free" books, but they hated the nature study part of Charlotte Mason education. I'm a nature kid myself. My family did a lot of camping when I was younger and I loved spending time outside. I loved Charlotte Mason, but my children didn't. They did like bugs but I just couldn't talk them into doing a nature study. It's important to consider not just the style a parent leans towards, but what fits your children as well.

Hands-on and Child-led Learning

Child-led learning often involves using unit studies, theme-based lessons around one topic. When my children were younger, we did a unit study on the Oregon Trail. We learned about history, geography, and art, all with an Oregon Trail theme.

A similar approach is delight directed learning, which allows you to follow the interests of the child. One of my children loved economics and studied it year after year in high school. He ended up with quite a few economics credits on his transcript. When I was in school, I was involved in choir every year; it was my passion. Other children enjoy photography or artwork every year of high school because that is their passion.

Un-schooling is another approach that encourages children to learn naturally. Unschoolers try to expose their children to as many rich learning situations as possible, so they will learn things naturally much the way adults do. Many unschoolers add in daily math lessons though, because they don't want their kids to have to catch up on their own, later.

Many unschoolers focus on education each and every day. In other words, they're not just letting their children play video games all day. Unschooling parents are project managers who encourage children to learn on purpose each day (and get their math lesson done!).

Unschooling is different from non-schooling. I have one friend who called herself an "ashamed non-schooler," because she told people she was an unschooler but wasn't doing anything at all. That's not recommended! Learning on purpose is recommended, regardless of what style you choose.

Many homeschoolers try to move away from a public school mentality as much as possible when they withdraw their child from a classroom setting; they spend some time de-schooling. Bullying at school or learning disabilities that put their children far below grade level may have forced them to start homeschooling. De-schooling can be especially beneficial for children who have been harmed by bad experiences in the public school system.

We pulled our children out of a public school setting to homeschool because of a failure on the part of that public school. However, my children were such academics that I knew I couldn't let them spend time with natural learning alone. My children would've been bored; I knew they needed a heavy-duty curriculum right away.

As with all things, you have to trust your gut instincts because you know your child best. You will know whether your child needs a time of de-schooling to separate from the public school mentality or whether your child has been so bored in public school that you need to feed them books so they can get back to delight directed learning – a love of learning they have lost in the public school setting. Listen to yourself and trust your own heart.

Worldview

Another kind of homeschool approach is based on worldview. One example is the Principle Approach. It focuses on values, and is faith-based, centering on God and country. This approach often focuses on American history year after year. The emphasis is on character and morality.

There's also secular homeschooling, for homeschoolers that want to avoid a religious curriculum. A difficulty secular homeschoolers sometimes face is the Christian heritage aspect of homeschooling. For decades, parents have homeschooled mostly because of their Christian worldview; much of the oldest, tried and true curriculum is based on a Christian worldview. Curriculum can be Catholic or Evangelical but they do tend to be religious in nature. I appreciate the struggle secular homeschoolers have to find a non-religious curriculum, but it's important to keep an open mind. Christian curriculum has been around for a long, time, is tried and true, homeschool friendly, and meant for homeschoolers. A Christian curriculum could be the best fit for your child even though it has a worldview you may not appreciate.

If you want to use a secular homeschool approach but like a Christian curriculum, you can remove certain parts of the curriculum that you don't find appropriate for your children. I do encourage you not to throw the baby out with the bath water; it may be that a Christian homeschool curriculum is still the best fit for your child.

Chapter 5

Learning Styles

Children have their own learning styles, just as parents have their own learning styles. I use pictures for everything I do because I'm a visual learner and I need visual feedback. They're a prompt for me, spur my thoughts, and help me think and learn.

Each Child is Unique

Each child is born with innate differences. They have personal preferences. Our job is to try to match their learning style to a curriculum, to improve their learning retention.

It's helpful to use multiple learning styles in your lessons. There are programs out there that incorporate all of the learning styles. The problem is it can take forever to teach a lesson in all four learning styles! If you teach history and engage in a hands-on activity, listen to audios, and watch videos, then each lesson may take forever! It's best to pick and choose which parts of the curriculum you want to use.

Our children are unique and that is why brick and mortar schools or online schools frustrate me. How can one kind of schooling adequately educate all children when each child is unique? It's like sending your exceedingly artistic child to MIT Engineering School or sending your gifted engineering-inclined kid to Cornell School of the Arts!

Learning Styles in a Nutshell

Some people are visual learners. They often say things like, "I see what you're saying" or "Look at this!" Listen to your children – do they use many visually focused words? Often that means they are visual learners.

Other people are auditory learners. They will often say, "I hear what you're saying" or "Listen to this" or "Listen to me." These kids are auditory learners and may do better by listening; they often have ear buds in their ears. I recommend the website "My Audio School" for lessons incorporating music that are great for auditory learners or kids who have learning challenges such as dyslexia.

Kinesthetic learners learn best through movement. Skiers, for example, are usually kinesthetic learners; they learn best through moving. They may use words like, "I get it, let's get going." These are kids who always touch things. One thing to remember about kinesthetic learners is that their desire for movement does not mean the itty-bitty movement of a pen or pencil on paper or typing at the computer. Their movement has to include the large muscles of the body, moving their legs and arms and not just their fingers!

Personality Influences

In addition to learning styles, there is also a child's personality to consider. Personality influences the way people behave. There are social learners who learn best when somebody is talking to them face to face. Sometimes they'll say they wish they had a teacher; it's not because they wish they were in a public school, rather, they like to learn face to face with somebody looking them in the eye. They will often focus on faces and learn best through interaction; this can be interaction with Mom, a face in a video with expressions they can read, or a friend to meet with for book discussions.

Children also have different temperaments. I have one child who's very slow to warm up. He likes to have a thorough understanding of things before he jumps in with both feet. As long as we gave him enough time to think about it, he was fine. Personality has a lot to do with multiple intelligences. There are many tests available to determine your child's personality type. Often you'll find the tests reveal what you already knew, so I don't usually recommend you spend money testing your children for multiple intelligences.

Learning readiness also varies from child to child. Some kids are ready to read at age eight, and other kids aren't ready until age 12. You can try and try from the time they're five, but if they're not ready until they're 12, it's like hitting your head against the wall!

Many parents will identify as the parent of a struggling learner. Sometimes the problem is not intelligence, dyslexia, or other learning challenges; sometimes the challenge is waiting for a child's brain to be ready to learn, waiting for a certain point of maturity.

I know a parent whose son was a struggling learner and started reading very late. She had to read everything to him. Then one day he went from not being able to read to suddenly being at grade level. It came as a surprise to her. I got the impression that she originally wondered whether it was her fault or whether she had done something wrong. Did she choose the wrong curriculum? In fact, it all boiled down to whether her child was ready to learn.

If you don't know where to begin with learning styles, tools, and curriculum, I recommend the Home Ed Expert website. They offer a long questionnaire, (which frustrates some people), but it will help you find specific curriculum suggestions based on your child's learning style. But always remember, you know your child best!

Chapter 6

Fads, Fears, and Peer Pressure

As parents, we are concerned about the peer pressure our children face, but the truth is that sometimes parents face peer pressure as well! We may look at our friends and wish we had done what they did. If anybody uses the words, "you should," they're applying peer pressure. Listen for this and pay attention. As the parent, you know best, you know what the right fit is for your child. Just because there's a new homeschool fad doesn't mean it's a good fit for your child.

Homeschoolers are concerned about the word "accreditation." It can freak them out. Homeschoolers can also be afraid of honors classes. In some homeschool communities, AP classes and AP tests are the fad. Providing a highly rigorous or overly rigorous curriculum can be a fad as well. Not everything will be a good fit for your child because children have their own unique weaknesses and strengths.

Sometimes you'll experience peer pressure from an older homeschooler who has outdated information. This can be especially true when they talk about accreditation or how you "have to" do something. Their information may have been accurate 10 to 20 years ago but is not applicable today.

Community College and Co-Ops

One homeschool fad right now seems to be community college dual enrollment. Homeschoolers often pressure their friends into going to community college, as if it's the only way to help gain admission into college after high school. Beware that community college is a rated R environment, and may not always be appropriate for your high school age children.

Another fad is joining homeschool co-ops. These can be a great fit, but sometimes parents pressure each other and think the only way to homeschool is by attending co-op classes; it's not necessary.

Classical Education and Parent Partner Programs

Another current fad is using the classical education method. For many homeschoolers, the classical method is not a good fit. It generally works well for the narrow subset of children who are academically minded, do well in school, and thrive with a heavy reading load. If your friends use this method and you hear about it a lot, that doesn't necessarily mean it will be a good fit for your children.

Alternative education, or parent partner programs (similar to online classes), are also popular. These are public school programs targeted to homeschool families, offering part-time to full-time classes. Some parents exert pressure on their friends and cause them to fear they are missing out if they don't use alternative education courses. Sometimes these public school programs are appropriate for your children, but not always. When considering parent partner programs, I encourage you to consider why you started homeschooling. If you started homeschooling because public school wasn't working or meeting your child's needs, why wasn't it working? Those are the same reasons why alternative education or online classes might not be a good fit for you.

Facing Fads

My job is to help people homeschool independently. I recognize the fact that I do have a bias. When people ask me about options such as alternative education, I can't provide guidance about where to find a good program. My mission is to empower and encourage families to homeschool independently.

Remember that fad does not mean the same as fit. When facing fads, remember you are the Chief Executive Officer of your children's education – you're the one in charge. Know your child and trust yourself and your own judgment. If you try something, you can stop if it doesn't work. If you find out a month into school that it isn't working for your child, you can withdraw your child at any time. You are responsible for your own child. You're not responsible for other people's children, or for whether or not a class has enough kids in it. If your friends engage in peer pressure, remember your true friends will love you whether you follow them or not. Use what works for your child and your family. The buck stops with you. Listen to the facts, make a decision based on your full understanding of the situation, and make a change if it doesn't work.

Chapter 7

Subject Specific Suggestions

Believe it or not, I don't like recommending specific curriculum! Every family and child is unique, so even if I suggest a curriculum, I don't know what's best for your child — you do! However, I can provide some general suggestions and starting places.

The Homeschool Transition

If you are new to homeschooling, read my article, "Homeschooling High School for Freaked Out and Terrified Parents." Many people start homeschooling feeling nervous and afraid. There are some common issues people face when they homeschool for the first time in high school.

Your child may be peer dependent and is used to having other kids around. They may be faced with self-esteem issues from being bullied, picked on, or labeled at school. Sometimes your child will suffer from burn out, will absolutely hate learning and won't be interested in school at all. Some students only have a familiarity with textbooks not with learning. When we took our own children out of school, we discovered they hadn't learned anything there. They read textbooks in school that were full of information they already knew. Homeschooling was the first time they had to learn something new.

I encourage you to choose a curriculum that works well for beginners, something that will "hold your hand" as you start. When I started homeschooling, I used the *Sonlight* curriculum. It's easy to use and it will hold your hand! It's something I recommend beginners look at first. It's not always a good fit, but it's a good place for you to start. Another curriculum that's good for beginners is *Around the World in 180 Days*. It doesn't include everything but it can be a good starting place. You also might want to consider a time of de-schooling first, taking a break from any formal schooling when you pull your child from school. This can help your student reclaim their love of learning.

English

You can purchase an all-in-one English curriculum, which includes both reading and writing activities each day. If your curriculum only covers writing, consider including some reading, too. If you have a curriculum that is just reading, likewise include some writing each day.

I encourage you to focus on your child's ability level rather than grade level. It's difficult to determine a grade level for English work. You can't say that a 4-sentence paragraph is at fourth grade level and a 5-sentence paragraph is at fifth grade level.

If you include some test prep that covers vocabulary, editing skills, and grammar, it will benefit your child. It's especially important to teach children how to write a quick essay in high school English class. It's a skill needed for taking tests in college.

Teaching grammar every year is not necessary; you can teach it just once. I usually recommend *Winston Grammar*. Yearly grammar used to be a homeschool fad, but I don't see it as much anymore.

English is a lot like math; it might take one hour a day at the beginning of high school. In math, students often get into calculus and find it can take two or three hours to complete a lesson each day. The same thing can happen in the upper years of high school English.

English Fun

Remember to have fun reading in your homeschool. Check out my website for some great book suggestions in my "College Bound Reading List."

Books that have been made into movies and movies that have been made into books can be a lot of fun to read and then you can watch the movie together as a reward. Sometimes, watching the movie first will enhance your student's interest in reading a book. You can include some audio books, so children who struggle with reading, especially dyslexic children, can still get the experience of reading many books, without the struggle. Audio books can also help students improve their vocabulary.

You can also include writing for fun, using online writing prompts. Consider having your child write for publication. Submit their writing to a literary magazine or encourage them to start their own blog.

Include some literary analysis if your children love it (some children do!), or skip it (as I did) if they don't. Don't feel you have to include it; it's okay to instill the love of reading and writing in your child and nothing more.

Curriculum Suggestions

There are great writing curriculum out there. The *Institute for Excellence in Writing* is what I used as well as the integrated curriculum from *Sonlight*. I found both of them helpful. *Write Shop*'s curriculum is also easy to use, as is *Brave Writer*'s.

When buying an English curriculum, remember that in this one area there can be a big payoff. If somebody paid you $40,000 in college scholarship money to write an English essay, you would probably write it. If you needed to, you would definitely buy that $100 curriculum so you could earn the $40,000 for writing one essay. Investing in a good English curriculum is worth it.

Math

In general, a video tutorial is an important key to math success. Whether your child is a visual learner or not, somebody has to explain upper math concepts. I don't know how much geometry you remember, but it can be a challenge for some people! It can also help to have access to answers from the curriculum provider, through either an online chat or a toll free phone number.

There are two generally used math sequences and homeschoolers have their own preferences about which to use. You can teach Geometry either before or after Algebra 2. Some homeschoolers like to use this sequence:

Pre-Algebra - Algebra 1 - Geometry - Algebra 2

Others like to use this order:

Pre-Algebra - Algebra 1 - Algebra 2 – Geometry

It probably doesn't matter which sequence you choose. Your goal is to try to get Geometry class completed before eleventh grade if possible. The PSAT test includes some geometry and your child will get a better score if they can get their Geometry class in before eleventh grade. If your child is going to take the

PSAT soon, try to include Geometry class before Algebra 2 class.

In each math curriculum, the number of practice problems varies widely. Some kids need to work on many practice problems before they understand a concept, and other kids will only need a few. If your child needs more math problems, you may need a book with more. If your child doesn't need many math problems to be successful, you're free not to cover all of the math problems in the book.

There are literature-based math curriculum out there, but many of them don't offer enough practice problems for the average child. If you use a literature-based math curriculum, you may need to supplement with more problems. For additional, higher-level math practice, look at SAT or ACT test prep books. They include problems for Algebra, Geometry, and Algebra 2 classes. Test prep books can provide the extra practice problems needed when you use a literature-based math curriculum or a curriculum that doesn't have as many problems as your child needs.

Math Curriculum

There are many different math programs out there.

Saxon is a top-rated math curriculum used by homeschoolers. It's supposed to be the best, but that doesn't mean it's the best fit for you. It doesn't matter how highly rated it is if your child hates it, because then your child won't learn from it. If you use a lesser rated program your child loves, they'll learn more than if you use something they hate. The nice thing about *Saxon* is that it does have many practice problems.

Because it is a top-rated homeschool curriculum, and because it's designed for homeschoolers, Saxon has three different companion video tutorials available. The *Saxon Teacher* videos are offered by *Saxon* itself. DIVE, a Christian company that coordinates with *Saxon*, has *DIVE into Saxon* DVDs available. Homeschool with Saxon also offers a *Saxon DVD Teaching Series*. If you look at *Saxon* and find it is the best choice for your child, look at each of these videos separately to decide which one is going to be perfect for your children.

Another standard math curriculum you'll see frequently through homeschool groups is *Teaching Textbooks*, which is very popular. It was created by Harvard graduates and is the perfect fit for some kids. Others find it visually distracting. As with any curriculum, it depends on personal preference.

VideoText has been around for a long time. Some homeschoolers are highly successful with it. It's difficult to speed up with this program, though, and it doesn't include many practice problems. It can be hard to go back over it again if your child doesn't understand it the first time. *Chalkdust* is similar, and it has been around for a long time. Make sure to check out the video. The same goes for the *Thinkwell* curriculum.

Math-U-See is a hands-on math program. Look carefully at it. *Math-U-See* tends to take a much different approach to math than other programs.

There's also a video series called *Ask Dr. Callahan*, which works with the Jacobs Textbooks (*Jacobs Algebra, Jacobs Geometry*). The Harold Jacobs' textbooks are extremely highly rated and for this reason, I think the *Ask Dr. Callahan* curriculum would be worth looking into. Back in my day, we didn't have *Ask Dr. Callahan* available and I was able to teach Algebra 1 and Geometry just using *Harold Jacobs' Algebra*. I was successful; it was an easy book to use. I'm not a math wizard and it was easy for me.

For school-at-home types, *A Beka* and *Bob Jones* might be good choices. *A Beka* is filmed in a classroom setting, which can tend to drive kids crazy because there will be questions from the classroom and you have to wait for the teacher to answer. It's very much a school-at-home style video.

There's also a newer, online curriculum called *ALEKS*. Many homeschoolers love it and it could be a great math curriculum for independent learners.

Again, make sure you look at each curriculum carefully. View the video tutorials together, because children have personal preferences we don't know about. Be aware if they think an instructor looks or sounds difficult to learn from.

Math Fun

Make sure you spend some time having fun with math. You can include math games or supplements. In the younger years, we used *Family Math*; there's also *Family Math for Middle School*. Towards the high school years, check out a program called *Patty Paper Geometry for* hands-on geometry experiments.

When you get into higher math levels, there's a great video I strongly encourage homeschoolers to see; part of *The Great Courses* series, it's called

Calculus Made Clear. We watched it when our children took Pre-Calculus, and we watched it again quite a few times when they took Calculus; my children loved it!

Another great supplement is *Khan Academy*, which is a free online video supplement. Public school kids use it all the time; if they don't understand part of their homework, they go to their website for clarification.

For younger children, there's a neat website called *Living Math*. It offers readers for math; you can read real, fun literature books about circumference, π, and many other math concepts. It has many ideas that are just wonderful, but most of them are for younger kids.

Social Studies

High school social studies usually includes world history, US history, economics, and government. These are subjects colleges look for on a transcript. Social studies can also include anything on the study of human behavior, such as sociology or psychology. There are many literature-based options, too. If your child likes to read, you have many things to look at and consider.

Tapestry of Grace (a complete curriculum that includes social studies) is extremely popular, as is *My Father's World*, and both are Christian curriculum. *Sonlight* curriculum is the one I used. *Beautiful Feet Books* offers great literature packs and study guides.

Veritas Press is a literature-based option for classical education. Some of their books are at the college level. Although this can sound like a good idea, be careful that your children aren't in over their heads with an advanced curriculum. Some of the *Veritas Press* books are ones my children read in the honors program as juniors in college. It may not be appropriate for every child to read those books at the high school level. *Truth Quest History* and *The Noah Plan* are also great options.

Fun with Social Studies

Remember that history books can overlap with English studies. *The Red Badge of Courage*, for example, is American literature, but it's American literature about the Civil War. That's going to cover both areas.

There is a great social studies curriculum that uses multiple learning styles (which is my favorite for kids who might not like to read or who want a variety of learning styles), called *History Revealed* by Diana Waring. If you have a researcher, *Around the World in 180 Days* is a great curriculum. If your child learns best with videos or movies, then consider looking at materials from *The Great Courses*. It can provide learning opportunities for kids who are visual learners or who need a little extra help. It can be a wonderful supplement.

For hands-on fun, have your children join a speech or debate club. Speech and debate can involve research about social studies. There are also many board games kids can play to encourage learning in specific areas. They can also build models of World War II ships or castles that can help them cement the time period they're learning about. Becoming involved in TeenPact, Youth & Government, or being a page at your state capital can also cement a student's knowledge about American government and economics in a fun way.

Science

There are science programs that cater to just about every learning style. An audio learner might do best with audio textbooks. *Apologia* has an MP3 download. There's also video curriculum available. If you're having trouble with a concept, go to *Khan Academy*. That's what public school kids and homeschoolers alike use when they don't understand a concept. You can access video supplements for concepts such as balancing chemical equations.

I recommend you include a lab with at least one of your high school sciences. However, there is no set definition for what a lab science means and not all colleges even require a lab. Usually when a college talks about science requirements, they don't require all science courses to include a lab. Make sure you investigate admission requirements of colleges where your child wants to apply. If your child wants to go to an engineering school, it's a good idea to include biology, chemistry, and physics classes, each with a lab. If you'd like more information on what a lab is (and isn't), and when it is (or isn't) necessary, read my article on The HomeScholar website, "You Can Teach Science Labs."

For lab materials, I recommend you go to *Home Science Tools* at www.hometrainingtools.com and check out their materials. They have lab materials for all sciences available. There are also curriculum options for sciences outside of biology, chemistry, or physics. If your child wants to learn about astronomy, ecology, or robotics, you will find curriculum there. *Home Science Tools* is a great source of science resources outside the normal path.

Fun with Science

If you want to pursue interest-led learning, 4-H clubs are popular and they're a great way to get your child interested in science. There are also robotics clubs, where kids get together and build robots. Science fairs and science clubs also cater to hands-on kids.

You can make your science labs more fun by inviting friends over to do science together. My children were very strong readers, so we used a textbook for science and then got together with our friends to do experiments. It worked great, and was more fun for everybody.

Foreign Language

One of the most important keys to success in foreign language is to practice every single day for at least 15 minutes. Even on bad days, put in 15 minutes. I've spoken to many different curriculum providers, and some have told me it doesn't matter which curriculum you use as long as you practice for 15 minutes every day; this has to do with how our brains are wired. If we don't use something for a few days, our brain can forget what it means, and we have to re-learn it.

There are several top-rated programs for foreign language. *Rosetta Stone* is internationally known. They have the largest number of languages available, even some of the more unusual ones.

Power Glide is the curriculum I used for French and it was exceedingly effective. We enjoyed using it. It can still be found at used bookstores. *Tell Me More* is another popular program. There are many options for Latin, but I recommend *The Latin Road to English Grammar*. I found it easy to use and I was completely terrified of Latin.

There are four different kinds of skills to learn when studying a foreign language: listening, speaking, reading, and writing. Not every curriculum has all of those pieces. Try to include some of each of those pieces when you teach your foreign language class. It's like teaching

English – you have to make sure you cover reading and writing. When you teach a foreign language, you have to teach listening, speaking, reading, and writing. Don't forget to include a study of the culture and geography. Homeschoolers don't always think about including them, but they put a foreign language in perspective.

Foreign Language Fun

One of the most fun ways to improve your foreign language is to watch movies in the language. Children's movies are at a lower vocabulary level and are easier to understand in a foreign language. We watched "Finding Nemo" in French and used subtitles! Sometimes we just listened to it in French so my children could learn to listen for the language. Other times we listened in English but turned on the French subtitles so they could learn to read in French. It was a great way for us to have fun!

Sometimes you can find volunteer organizations that serve people who speak your foreign language. If there's a large Hispanic community near you, maybe you can volunteer with a Hispanic support organization and practice Spanish.

Setting Facebook to an alternate language and playing video games in a foreign language can also be fun. Watch Spanish language channels on TV. Enjoy language-learning apps on your digital device. Another good resource to look into is *Livemocha*, which is an online community where people agree to teach one another their own language. Of course, be careful anytime you get into an online community, since there could be risks involved.

Another way to have fun with foreign language is to incorporate crafts and recipes into your class. In high school, I took Russian and French. In both classes, we spent quite a bit of time crafting and doing recipes. I remember making crepes and Ukrainian eggs. These are important ways to have fun learning a foreign language and understanding the culture. If you can, travel is also a great way to learn a new language!

Physical Education

Physical education doesn't have to be taught using a curriculum, which means you get to save money! You can teach PE naturally with no curriculum at all and include things such as health, nutrition, fitness, or first aid. You can include books, but you don't have to. When I took PE in public school, it didn't include any books. You can make your courses health-focused, but make sure to focus on your children's long-term health. Alternatively, you can base PE on exercise that is more physical. Anything that breaks a sweat can count for your physical education program!

Some activities involve physical fitness. The Congressional Award program provides awards for physical fitness and volunteer work. Scouting, especially becoming an Eagle Scout, is a great way to get involved in, and receive rewards for, physical fitness.

Sometimes people get confused about what a physical education class might include. The options are broad. When I was in PE in public school, one of our activities was archery. It may be scary now to think about kids pointing arrows at each other, but I did that in high school. If an event is included in the Olympics, it can count as PE in homeschool. If your child goes shooting on a gun range, participates in equestrian events, or skiing, their activity can be counted as PE. Remember to include anything that breaks a sweat!

Fine Arts

Fine Arts is another area where curriculum is generally not required. The fine arts include music, art, theater, and dance. You can blend it altogether and call that your fine arts class. Not everybody likes music, art, theater, and dance, though. Some of your friends go to the theater, while others wouldn't be caught dead there. Some people are very musical, and some are very quiet and don't like listening to music.

For a technology-inclined student, you could teach fine arts by having them take digital photography. Often kids that don't like fine arts have great technical skills. Techies like the computer and are willing to do digital photography since it's computer-based.

If your bookish child doesn't like the fine arts, you can teach them using books. Learn about art by reading about its history or do a composer or artist study.

Private or group instrumental or vocal lessons are another option. You can delegate your fine arts class and have your child take lessons with a teacher.

Try different learning style approaches for fun. Sometimes your child will do an activity for fun and you won't even realize it's fine arts! Maybe they're involved in crafting and do a lot of sewing or knitting. You can count it for fine arts credit. Look for fun in lessons or join 4-H. Look around at the tools and supplies in your home. Remember, a curriculum is not required for the fine arts.

Electives

Electives are also courses that don't usually require a curriculum. Electives can include a couple of different categories. They might include your own family requirements. Maybe in your family, you require auto mechanics or critical thinking. Sometimes your state will have strange elective requirements. My state requires occupational education. Check out your state requirements.

One of your electives might include test preparation. The studying your child does for test prep could be a class called "Study Skills." Again, curriculum is not required.

Electives can be put together through delight directed learning. Think about what your children do for fun, about what they do that annoys you. My son loves chess, and his constantly playing chess annoyed me. Many of his electives were chess-related. Sometimes his chess activities counted as a critical thinking credit and sometimes public speaking. Occupational education definitely was earned through his chess playing! Look at your "annoy-o-meter" and think about what your child does that bugs you and whether it might become an elective.

Remember that not all classes have to be difficult. When we were in high school, we referred to some classes as "underwater basket weaving." I took a class in high school called Polynesian History and all of my friends laughed about it because it was such an easy class. It's important to recognize that not all classes have to be difficult; it's okay for some of our classes to be easier.

Fun School Ideas

Although it's important to make sure you cover core classes carefully (which means math, science, English, and history), sometimes you can cover them in a fun way. Of course, you can mix in any fluff and fun with the more serious subjects. Fun can always add interest to a curriculum. Anything you can do to make your child's courses more interesting can help them learn.

4-H might count as art or it might bring some excitement to your child's science classes. If your child is an Eagle Scout, all of their badges might count towards PE, art, leadership, or technology. Some families have a rich, cultural heritage. You can study the culture and language of your family of origin. There are always award programs and competitions to get involved in, too. The Congressional Award mentioned above in the PE section is a great opportunity to pursue for fun.

Fun School Stuff

One homeschool student I know was heavily involved in cartooning. There's information available online about cartooning, such as tutorials on how to draw cartoons and comics. The Harold Jacobs' math book has cartoons all the way through it! Cartoonists often begin drawing because they like the Japanese style of anime. Sometimes you can talk these students into studying Japanese for their foreign language. They may get a bit more excited when they can say "oof!" or "pow!" with their cartoons and comics because they know the Japanese language, so it makes it more fun for them.

Another crazy, fun example is learning with movies. Teach with Movies is a website where you can look at movies through history that will visually express the time period you're learning about. Mix the fluff and the fun into your day, because although you do have to cover the core classes, you can still make it enjoyable.

This is a brief overview of some of my subject specific recommendations. Included in my *Coffee Break Book* Series are titles that cover specific subject areas in much greater depth.

Visit my Amazon author page to see all my current books.

amazon.com/author/leebinz

Chapter 8

Money Matters: Cost of Curriculum

The cost of the curriculum does matter, and it can be frustratingly expensive. If you are choosing a new curriculum, do a real comparison between the latest and greatest versus the tried and true. People often want the newest thing — it has to be shiny, cool, and brand new. Usually it's the tried and true that's better and that you'll be able to purchase used. You don't have to feel badly if you don't get the shiny new textbook. You can get the tried and true. Often, hands-on learning will be a more cost-effective approach. If you teach an art class, a PE class, or an elective class, you can save a lot of money by not paying for curriculum in those areas.

When thinking about a curriculum, do a cost-benefit analysis. A cost-benefit analysis is a determination of whether something will pay off in the long run. What is the long-term investment?

It will pay off to spend money on English and math curriculum. Many other subjects can be learned naturally — you can go to the library or you can watch free movies on TV. In general, you need to invest in a math book so your child will learn math concepts, put math on their transcript, get scholarships, and then earn a good score on the ACT or SAT. A cost-benefit analysis needs to pay off. Likewise, investing in English curriculum will pay off. Your student's ability to express herself in writing will lead to good college scholarships. Writing skills will help students get good grades in college, which can lead to good jobs out of college. When you do a cost-benefit analysis, look at the long-term investment, particularly in math and English – the skills for college and for life. It's okay to pay real money for great curriculum, especially in those areas that represent a long-term investment.

The curriculum you buy usually has a copyright on it and it's there for a reason. Don't make copies and distribute them to your friends. When you buy a curriculum, it's your curriculum and it belongs to you. You can give away (or in most cases sell) the whole curriculum, but you can't copy it and give your friends a copy. Breaking a copyright protection in order to save money on a curriculum is not an option.

Chapter 9

Other Resources

For deciding on curriculum, my favorite book is *102 Top Picks for Homeschool Curriculum* by Cathy Duffy. You can find many of her reviews on her website as well. One of the benefits of referring to her book is that you know for a fact the curriculum listed is tried and true; it has been around long enough to be in her book. Cathy Duffy helped create the *Home Ed Expert*, which is a tool to help assess your child's learning styles. It can be a tedious process, so if you have a feel for your children's learning styles already, going directly to the Cathy Duffy reviews website or reading her book is probably faster and easier.

Look to the experts when you want to read reviews. It's okay to read what your friends and bloggers suggest, but bloggers are not expert reviewers. They may not understand the nuances of what should be included in a geography class, or how far trigonometry should go before calling it Pre-Calculus. It is good to look at what other people like, just understand that those are personal opinions from friends and bloggers you see online. Personal opinions vary quite a bit and can still help you as you search through different choices, but make sure to look at the experts' opinions, too.

Appendix 1

Are You Doing Too Much?

Are you doing too much? It's a temptation when parents feel stressed about high school. Some parents tend to go overboard with the homeschool workload. Is that you? At first, parents just aren't sure what homeschool high school should look like. Then in sophomore and junior year, in a panic over college, they pile even more work on their already overworked child. By the time senior year comes around, it gets even worse as they race to fill in perceived gaps from the first few years of high school. Does this sound a bit like your homeschool? Let's take a step back, and try to look at the bigger picture.

Consider your expectations. Try to seek some balance.

The Consequences

Piling on the work out of panic won't help. Expecting too much causes anxiety and conflict between you and your child. Add this to a time when your teen is yearning for independence, and it's a recipe for disaster. The high school years aren't the time to panic and pile on the work just because college is looming. Kids need free time as well, to ensure a peaceful home instead of a tumultuous one. They will learn more when they aren't stressed.

My Story of Excess

I've been there. I've made that mistake. It wasn't pretty. During freshman year, I demanded far too much from my teens. My first year of high school included this long list: *The Latin Road to English Grammar 3, Jacob's Geometry, Patty Paper Geometry, Apologia Chemistry, Power Glide French 1, Sonlight American History,* a *Teaching*

Company History course, current events, timeline, mapping, *Learn to Write the Novel Way, Sonlight Language Arts*, journal writing, *Sonlight* literature with literary analysis, read-aloud books, dictation, analogies, *Spelling Power*, piano, composer, poet, and artist of the month with reports, Bible study workbook, scripture memorization, and personal devotions.

Phew! It makes my heart race to read over that again. We crashed and burned in just a month. We couldn't get it all done. Shocking, I know! Each resource, curriculum, and idea in this list is just wonderful, with educational opportunities galore. It was simply too much at once.

Too Many Supplements

Are you using too many curriculum supplements in your homeschool? Can you spot the supplements in the list above? *Patty Paper Geometry, The Teaching Company* courses, current events, spelling, dictation, analogies, journal writing, scripture memorization, and composers, artists, and poet study were all supplements. Beware! You could even be supplementing the supplements!

Don't Double Up

Are you doubling up on a subject? We were! We studied two different foreign languages: French and Latin. We discussed how difficult it would be, but my kids WANTED to study both and were highly motivated, so I knew that in advance. What I didn't realize right away was that I was using two, separate, full-year English programs: *Learn to Write the Novel Way* and *Sonlight Language Arts*. Not only that, but I was supplementing those two English curriculum with multiple supplements!

Relax and let your wings be lifted with your child's delight in learning, at a slower pace.

Just Say No

After the first month, I became worried about both my children's attitudes. They seemed lazy, unmotivated, and worked so slowly! I sat down with my husband and we took the list and started cutting it down. We cut out some great programs and activities; it was so hard to say no to them. There just wasn't enough time in the day and something had to go. We made sure we kept the "big rocks," the core classes and those required for college admission. Then we sprinkled in a little bit of fun, supplemental fluff on top, the "sand," that still had room to fit.

Make Changes

How many subjects are you covering in your homeschool? English and math may take more than an hour each day, but none of the other subjects should. In fact, studies show that for maximum learning retention, each class should last no more than 50 minutes. Add everything up – how much are you expecting per day? Keep your child challenged, not overwhelmed. Remind yourself not to let your eyes get bigger than your stomach. Re-evaluate your plan mid-year, just in case you creep back into the habit of doing too much.

Learn from the Birds

I have a lifelong love affair with birds. In particular, I love hummingbirds. I squeal whenever I see one outside my kitchen window. If you've had a chance to observe them, have you ever noticed that hummingbirds flap their wings fastest when hovering in one place? Homeschoolers do that sometimes. They try to work so hard and fast that they accomplish less. If you try to do too much, your child could end up standing still! Although hummingbirds look adorable, they are quite violent and aggressive birds. Perhaps they are all stressed out from the flapping. Are you feeling stressed out, angry, frustrated, and burned out? Maybe you're like a hummingbird right now – flapping your wings furiously and not getting anywhere.

In contrast, have you ever watched a bald eagle in the air? Unlike hummingbirds, they don't flap much at all and they cover a lot of territory. You can't do it all. No one can. Soar a little like the bald eagle. Relax and let your wings be lifted with your child's delight in learning, at a slower pace.

Appendix 2

7 Point Reality Checklist for the New School Year

After homeschooling in the new school year for a month or two, it's a good time for a reality check! Keep what's working in your homeschool, throw out what's not working, and replace it with a new curriculum or new methods. Review this list and have your own homeschool reality check!

1. Is it working?

Is your math curriculum working? How about Spanish? If it's working, keep it. If it's not, re-evaluate it and try to determine why. For instance, if you're using a computer-based math curriculum and your child loves pencil and paper math (as my son did), perhaps you need to switch to a pencil and paper curriculum.

2. Are there enough hours in the day?

Did you purchase too much curriculum? Are you trying to cram 18 hours per day worth of curriculum into your homeschool day? If you had lofty goals and it's some fantastic curriculum, that's great! But perhaps you need to put some aside for next year. Sit down and chat with your child about what you can work on next year instead. Or maybe you need to drop some subjects completely – do you need to be studying TWO foreign languages or is one sufficient?

3. Is there too much curriculum?

It's impossible to do everything and all subjects all the time. I'm sure you bought 18 different kinds of curriculum at your last homeschool convention, and that's great! But you may need to thin it out to a reasonable level. What matters is what you do with your curriculum.

Cover the core classes of reading, writing, math, history, and science. If you can fit in foreign language, PE, fine arts and electives, that's great! But don't try to do it all plus 10 other things, because that's a recipe for disaster.

4. Are you expecting too much?

Are you expecting too much and demanding perfection from your child? They don't have to be perfect to demonstrate mastery of a subject. Mastery means your child understands a concept before you move on. Perfection is only possible for God, who is always right. I understand wanting to have high expectations, just try to steer clear of perfection and strive for mastery instead.

5. Are you forgetting life?

Part of your job is to make sure your child is ready for life, for leaving the nest. Remember to include life skills such as cooking, cleaning, and balancing a checkbook in your homeschool. Make learning these important life skills part of home economics or accounting credits.

6. Is technology a stumbling block?

Are technological gadgets distracting your children too much? Are video games taking up all of your teen's time? Is your teen turning into a zombie? You need to set clear boundaries on technology so children have the time, energy, and ability to get schoolwork and life skills done. Check out my article, "TechnoLogic: Setting Logical Boundaries on Technology with Your Teen" for some help on setting reasonable rules for your home and homeschool.

7. Reward success

While you're giving yourself a reality check, make sure you give yourself a pat on the back for what IS working in your homeschool. Remember, you're not a failure because some things aren't working, just change what's not working and move on for a great homeschool year!

Afterword

Who is Lee Binz and What Can She Do for Me?

Number one best-selling homeschool author, Lee Binz is The HomeScholar. Her mission is "helping parents homeschool high school." Lee and her husband Matt homeschooled their two boys, Kevin and Alex, from elementary through high school.

Upon graduation, both boys received four-year, full tuition scholarships from their first choice university. This enables Lee to pursue her dream job - helping parents homeschool their children through high school.

On The HomeScholar website, you will find great products for creating homeschool transcripts and comprehensive records to help you amaze and impress colleges.

Find out why Andrew Pudewa, Director of the Institute for Excellence in Writing says, "Lee Binz knows how to navigate this often confusing and frustrating labyrinth better than anyone."

You can find Lee online at:

www.TheHomeScholar.com

If this book has been helpful, could you please take a minute to write us a quick review on Amazon?

Thank you!

Testimonials

Full 4-Year Scholarship

"Dear Lee,

Thank you so much for the wealth of information that you share! You have given me the knowledge and courage to do more than I ever felt possible, especially the ability to maneuver the high school transcript and college application process. Our daughter was accepted to all six schools to which she applied. She was offered various scholarships to each of them, and she received a full four-year scholarship at the best school of all. This scholarship covers the full cost of tuition, room and board ... for all four years. Needless to say, we could not be happier! You gave me the courage to guide my daughter to write letters to admissions, scholarship and financial aid offices at each college. I am certain this made the difference. Thank you for everything!"

~ Lori in NH

Amazing Reception of our Transcript and Course Descriptions!

"My daughter was not only accepted to the one and only school she applied, but she was offered the highest scholarship they award and invited to join their honors program. That was wonderful news in and of itself but what happened at the Accepted Student's day yesterday is the reason for this email.

While in the parents meeting one of the administrators praised the transcript we sent in. They said it was the best one they had seen, and that perhaps I should teach a class. His comment was so unexpected, but I know that I thought, "teach a class, no. I took a class and my teacher was Lee Binz!"

Because I wanted clarification, I asked if it was the transcript or the course descriptions? The other administrator that is in charge of homeschooler applications, chimed in and said, "Oh, yeah, that was wonderful. The whole thing. Your descriptions of all the classes, that was great."

I recommend your program to anyone that asks. I tell them that you have so much more than just the book, and that if I had known, I would have bought your products sooner."

~ Aleyne in Maine

For more information about my **Total Transcript Solution** and **Comprehensive Record Solution**, go to:

www.TotalTranscriptSolution.com and www.ComprehensiveRecordSolution.com

Also From The HomeScholar...

- The HomeScholar Guide to College Admission and Scholarships: Homeschool Secrets to Getting Ready, Getting In and Getting Paid (Book and Kindle Book)
- Setting the Records Straight - How to Craft Homeschool Transcripts and Course Descriptions for College Admission and Scholarships (Book and Kindle Book)
- Preparing to Homeschool High School (DVD)
- Finding a College (DVD)
- The Easy Truth About Homeschool Transcripts (Kindle Book)

- Parent Training A la Carte (Online Training)
- Total Transcript Solution (Online Training, Tools and Templates)
- Comprehensive Record Solution (Online Training, Tools and Templates)
- Gold Care Club (Comprehensive Online Support and Training)
- Homeschool "Convention at Home" Kit (Book, DVDs and Audios)

The HomeScholar "Coffee Break Books" Released or Coming Soon on Kindle and Paperback:

- Delight Directed Learning: Guiding Your Homeschooler Toward Passionate Learning
- Creating Transcripts for Your Unique Child: Help Your Homeschool Graduate Stand Out from the Crowd
- Beyond Academics: Preparation for College and for Life
- Planning High School Courses: Charting the Course Toward High School Graduation
- Graduate Your Homeschooler in Style: Make Your Homeschool Graduation Memorable

- Keys to High School Success: Get Your Homeschool High School Started Right!
- Getting the Most Out of Your Homeschool This Summer: Learning just for the Fun of it!
- Finding a College: A Homeschooler's Guide to Finding a Perfect Fit
- College Scholarships for High School Credit: Learn and Earn With This Two-for-One Strategy!
- College Admission Policies Demystified: Understanding Homeschool Requirements for Getting In
- A Higher Calling: Homeschooling High School for Harried Husbands (by Matt Binz, Mr. HomeScholar)
- Gifted Education Strategies for Every Child: Homeschool Secrets for Success
- College Application Essays: A Primer for Parents
- Creating Homeschool Balance: Find Harmony Between Type A and Type Zzz...
- Homeschooling the Holidays: Sanity Saving Strategies and Gift Giving Ideas
- Your Goals this Year: A Year by Year Guide to Homeschooling High School

- Making the Grades: A Grouch-Free Guide to Homeschool Grading
- High School Testing: Knowledge That Saves Money
- Getting the BIG Scholarships: Learn Expert Secrets for Winning College Cash!
- Easy English for Simple Homeschooling: How to Teach, Assess and Document High School English
- Scheduling - The Secret to Homeschool Sanity: Plan You Way Back to Mental Health
- Junior Year is the Key to High School Success: How to Unlock the Gate to Graduation and Beyond
- Upper Echelon Education: How to Gain Admission to Elite Universities
- How to Homeschool College: Save Time, Reduce Stress and Eliminate Debt
- Homeschool Curriculum that's Effective and Fun: Avoid the Crummy Curriculum Hall of Shame!
- Comprehensive Homeschool Records: Put Your Best Foot Forward to Win College Admission and Scholarships
- Options After High School: Steps to Success for College or Career

- How to Homeschool 9th and 10th Grade: Simple Steps for Starting Strong!
- Senior Year Step-by-Step: Simple Instructions for Busy Homeschool Parents
- High School Math The Easy Way: Simple Strategies for Homeschool Parents In Over Their Heads

Would you like to be notified when we offer the next *Coffee Break Books* for FREE during our Kindle promotion days? If so, leave your name and email below and we will send you a reminder.

http://www.TheHomeScholar.com/freekindlebook.php

Visit my Amazon Author Page!

amazon.com/author/leebinz

Made in the USA
Lexington, KY
18 August 2017